imagine quilts

11 patterns from everyday inspirations

DANA BOLYARD

DEDICATION

To my husband and daughters, of course, for giving me the encouragement, freedom and time to chase my dreams. I love you.

Imagine Quilts: 11 Patterns from Everyday Inspirations
© 2014 by Dana Bolyard

Martingale®
19021 120th Ave. NE, Ste. 102
Bothell, WA 98011-9511 USA
ShopMartingale.com

Printed in China
19 18 17 16 15 14   8 7 6 5 4 3 2 1

5578 4804
9/14

Library of Congress Cataloging-in-Publication Data is available upon request.

ISBN: 978-1-60468-409-4

MISSION STATEMENT

Dedicated to providing quality products and service to inspire creativity.

CREDITS

PRESIDENT AND CEO: Tom Wierzbicki
EDITOR IN CHIEF: Mary V. Green
DESIGN DIRECTOR: Paula Schlosser
MANAGING EDITOR: Karen Costello Soltys
ACQUISITIONS EDITOR: Karen M. Burns
TECHNICAL EDITOR: Rebecca Kemp Brent
COPY EDITOR: Melissa Bryan
PRODUCTION MANAGER: Regina Girard
COVER AND INTERIOR DESIGNER: Connor Chin
PHOTOGRAPHER: Brent Kane
ILLUSTRATOR: Missy Shepler

contents

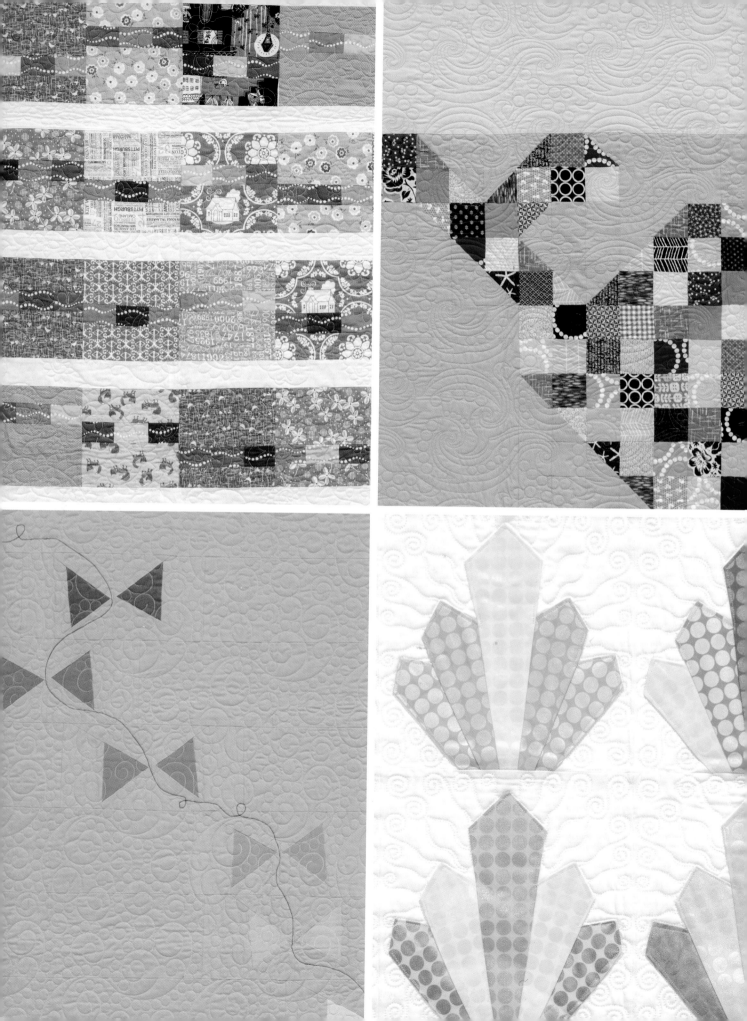

introduction

I've never been a pattern-based sewist; usually, I have an idea for a project and then find a way to make it. Scale drawings, scribbled mathematical computations, colored pencils, graph paper, and lots of wrinkled brows and head scratching have always been part of my process. Inspiration can come from anywhere: water droplets on a leaf, colors in the recycle bin, a favorite quote, a threadbare sweater in need of repair. Once I get an idea, I can't shake it. I sketch, map, and figure until my rotary blade starts spinning and my sewing machine humming.

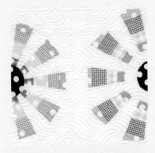

This book will spur your imagination and help you start turning your own quilt ideas into reality. On each page of the book I try to point your compass in a direction that lets you see not only how to find inspiration, but also how to turn an idea into a quilt.

The first section turns your creative attention toward your own fabric stash. Pull your fabric out, move it around, put it into random stacks, and see where it leads you. The second section suggests using a well-known technique in a new and unexpected way. While the projects focus specifically on making Dresden Plate wedges, what about Y-seam, flying-geese, or prairie-point techniques used in new ways? The third section asks you to look around at your daily life and see all the inspiration that abounds. The fourth section gives you permission to break the rules with three quilts that could inspire many more.

This book shows you how my creative process works. I invite you to grab some graph paper and discover how your own process works!

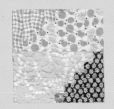

be inspired by your stash

I don't always have a specific project in mind when I buy fabric. If I see a print that I love, I usually buy a fat quarter, knowing I'll find a use for it soon enough. Sometimes when I'm feeling uninspired—or overly industrious—I start a mass cleanup of my sewing area and quickly become sidetracked by all the new fabric combinations I see and all the ideas racing through my head.

Take a trip through your fabric stash sometime. I bet you'll be inspired, too.

elephant parade

Designed and pieced by Dana Bolyard; machine quilted by Russ Adams
Finished quilt: 84½" x 92½" • **Finished block:** 7" x 7"

If you're anything like me, some days you have more fabric in your stash than you know what to do with. Sometimes I'll look through my stash, pull out fabrics, rearrange, and be inspired by what I discover. One day I realized that I had an abundance of gray fabrics. As that stack of grays grew and wanted to topple over, I was struck by the thought of elephants, and "Elephant Parade" was born.

MATERIALS

Yardage is based on 42"-wide fabric.

30 fat quarters of assorted gray prints for blocks

1 fat quarter *each* of 9 assorted bright prints for blocks

1¾ yards of white solid for sashing

¾ yard of gray print for binding

7¾ yards of fabric for backing

92" x 100" piece of batting

Fabric Selection

For this quilt I used the same print in nine different bright colors so that the stripes on the gray "elephants" would be cohesive. I chose colors that made me think of India and festive elephant parades. Feel free to create your own mix of bright prints and colors.

CUTTING

From *each* of the gray fat quarters, cut:
4 squares, 8" x 8" (120 total)

From *each* of the bright fat quarters, cut:
7 strips, 2" x 21"; crosscut into 40 rectangles, 2" x 3" (360 total)

From the white solid, cut:
24 strips, 2½" x 42"

From the gray print for binding, cut:
9 strips, 2½" x 42"

PIECING THE BLOCKS

1. Sew three bright rectangles together end to end to make an 8" strip. Press the seam allowances to one side. Make 120.

Make 120.

2. Select an 8" gray square and use a rotary cutter and ruler to cut the square randomly into two pieces. No measuring is necessary, and the square need not be cut perfectly in half. The angle can be slightly wonky (not parallel to an edge), but don't make it too extreme or you won't be able to square up the block. If the gray print is directional, keep that in mind when making this cut.

3. Sew a pieced strip of bright fabrics between the two parts of the gray square. Press the seam allowances toward the gray fabric.

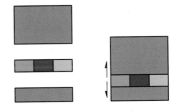

4. Repeat steps 2 and 3 to make 120 blocks. As you cut and sew the remaining blocks, vary the position of the cut across each gray square. Trim each block to 7½" x 7½".

ASSEMBLING THE QUILT TOP

1. Arrange 12 blocks into a row, varying the position of the brightly colored patchwork to achieve an irregular line of color across the row. Sew the blocks together, and press the seam allowances in one direction. Make 10 rows, pressing the seam allowances in alternate directions from row to row.

Make 10.

2. Remove the selvages and sew two white 2½"-wide strips together to make a sashing strip; make 11. Measure the length of each sashing strip; they must be 84½" long to fit the pieced rows. If your sashing strips are shorter, use the remaining white 2½"-wide strips to add length as necessary.

3. Arrange the pieced rows and sashing strips as shown in the quilt assembly diagram.

4. Find the center of each sashing strip and pin it to the bottom of the adjacent pieced row, pinning at the seam between the sixth and seventh blocks in the row. Then pin each end of the sashing strip to the corresponding end of the pieced row, easing any extra fabric into place as necessary. Sew the pinned rows together, and press the seam allowances toward the sashing.

5. Sew the block-and-sashing rows together. Stitch the remaining sashing strip to the top edge of the top row to complete the quilt top.

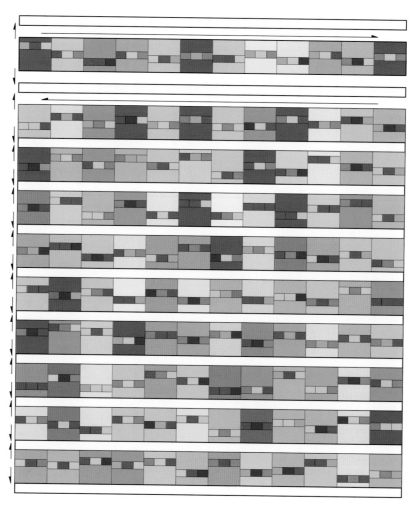

Quilt assembly

FINISHING THE QUILT

1. Cut the backing fabric into three 93"-long pieces. Remove the selvages and sew the pieces together side by side. Press the seam allowances open.

2. Layer the backing, batting, and quilt top. Refer to "Basting" on page 61 and baste the layers together.

3. Quilt as desired. The sample project features paisley quilting reminiscent of henna tattoos popular in India during festive occasions, which seems fitting for an elephant-inspired quilt. Trim the backing and batting to match the quilt top.

4. Referring to "Binding" on page 62, use the gray 2½"-wide strips to bind the quilt.

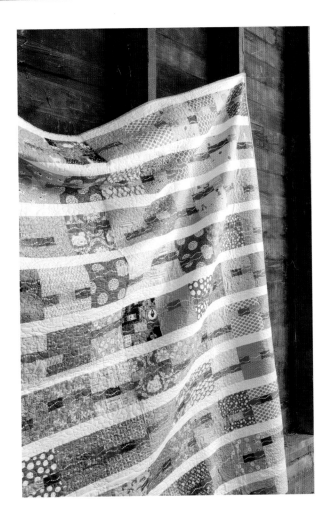

warm and cool log cabin

Designed and pieced by Dana Bolyard; machine quilted by Russ Adams
Finished quilt: 77" x 85½"   •   **Finished block:** 8½" x 8½"

*T*he humble Log Cabin block is divided diagonally, perfect for contrasting fabrics, and is traditionally made using light and dark prints. This version uses warm and cool hues for contrast instead of light and dark values. You need not pay attention to whether a fabric is light or dark, only whether the color is warm or cool.

*W*hen selecting fabrics for this quilt, choose fabrics that clearly fall into either the warm or cool category. If a fabric has contrasting elements that make it hard to categorize, save it for another project.

MATERIALS

Yardage is based on 42"-wide fabric.

⅛ yard *each* of 90 assorted warm-hued fabrics for blocks

⅛ yard *each* of 90 assorted cool-hued fabrics for blocks

¼ yard of red print for block centers

¾ yard of dark-blue print for binding

7⅛ yards of fabric for backing

84½" x 93" piece of batting

Wide Backings

It has become increasingly easy to find 108"-wide fabrics made for quilt backings. If you use a 108"-wide backing, recalculate the amount of yardage required for your project, using the batting size in the materials list as a guide. For "Warm and Cool Log Cabin," you'll need just 2½ yards of 108"-wide backing fabric.

CUTTING

The cutting instructions allow a little extra from each of the fabrics. If you make a mistake, you'll be prepared; if you don't, you'll have some precut strips to add to your scrap basket for your next project.

From *each* of the warm-hued fabrics, cut:

2 strips, 1½" x 42" (180 total)*

From *each* of the cool-hued fabrics, cut:

2 strips, 1½" x 42" (180 total)*

From the red print, cut:

90 squares, 1½" x 1½"

From the dark-blue print, cut:

9 strips, 2½" x 42"

*If you're piecing the quilt from scraps, cut at least four strips, 1½" x 18", from each of 90 warm- and 90 cool-hued fabrics.

PIECING THE BLOCKS

This block is constructed by adding strips ("logs") sequentially around the red center square.

1. Select a pair of matching warm strips, a pair of matching cool strips, and a 1½" red square for each block.

2. Remove the selvages from the strips and begin adding logs in numerical order as shown; the red square is number 1. Note that the warm-hued logs will all be added to the right and bottom of the red center, while the cool-hued logs will be added to the left and above the red center.

   Align the red square on one end of a warm-hued strip, right sides together. Sew along the red square's edge. Trim the strip to match the square and press the unit open, pressing the seam allowances toward the strip (the log).

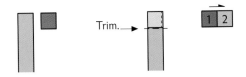

3. Position the assembled unit on one end of a warm strip, right sides together, and sew. Trim and press, turning the seam allowances toward the newly added log.

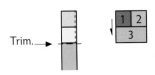

Pressing Pointer

Careful pressing after adding each new log will help ensure that the block stays square. You may also trim as necessary to square up the block.

4. Align the unit from step 3 with one end of a cool-hued strip, orienting the unit as shown. Stitch with right sides together. Trim and press toward the newly added log as before.

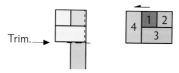

5. Continue adding, trimming, and pressing strips until you have added four logs to each side of the center square. Each block should measure 9" x 9". Make 90.

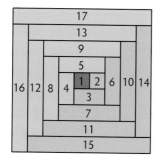

Make 90.

ASSEMBLING THE QUILT TOP

Once your blocks are complete, you have many choices for the design of your quilt layout. The sample quilt uses the Straight Furrows (also known as Fields and Furrows) setting, in which the blocks are arranged with the warm and cool fabrics forming diagonal lines. See "Design Options" on page 15 for more ideas, or create your own unique setting.

1. Arrange the blocks in your chosen setting, creating 10 rows of nine blocks each. Sew the blocks together into rows, and press the seam allowances in alternate directions from row to row.

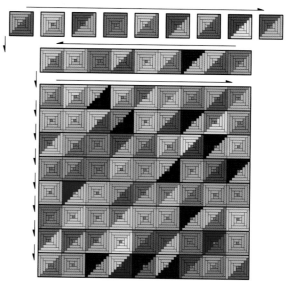

Fields and Furrows

2. Pin and sew the rows together to complete the quilt top. Press the seam allowances in one direction.

FINISHING THE QUILT

1. Cut the backing fabric into three 85½"-long pieces. Remove the selvages and sew the pieces together side by side. Press the seam allowances open. Trim the backing to 84½" x 93" if desired.

2. Layer the backing, batting, and quilt top. Refer to "Basting" on page 61 and baste the layers together.

3. Quilt as desired. I chose a quilting motif placed diagonally across the quilt to accentuate the diagonal design made by the warm and cool hues. An all-over quilting design would be lovely as well. Trim the backing and batting to match the quilt top.

4. Referring to "Binding" on page 62, use the dark-blue strips to bind the quilt.

Design Options

The traditional Log Cabin block offers so many arrangement options. Because the blocks have strong diagonal contrast, you can employ any of these traditional settings or create one that's all your own.

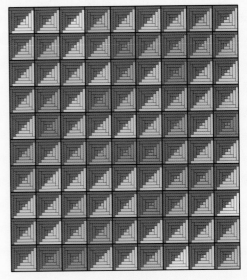

Straight Set

Streak of Lightning or Zigzag

Pinwheels

Barn Raising Variation

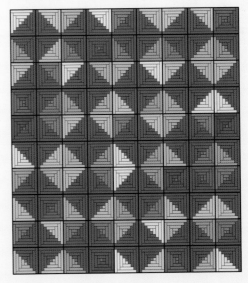

Sunshine and Shadow

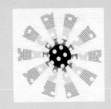  

use techniques in new ways

Quilting involves all sorts of specialized techniques and tools. But what about using a tried-and-true (or traditional or common) technique in a whole new way? This section takes the usual tricks for making Dresden Plate wedges and uses them in unexpected and innovative ways. Just let yourself think outside of the box.

Maybe there isn't even a box. . . .

three wheeling

Designed and pieced by Dana Bolyard; machine quilted by Russ Adams
Finished quilt: 63" x 87"

use techniques in new ways

*R*emember the pinwheels you played with as a child? You know—the ones on a stick, that twirled as you blew on them or held them high on a windy day? I wanted to make those in quilt form. The result is wonky, whimsical, and full of spin!

MATERIALS

Yardage is based on 42"-wide fabric.

4⅝ yards of white solid for background

¼ yard *or* 1 fat quarter of black polka dot for pinwheel centers

¼ yard *each* of 2 assorted bright prints (colors 2 and 6) for pinwheel wedges

⅛ yard *each* of 6 assorted bright prints (colors 1, 3, 4, 5, 7, and 8) for pinwheel wedges

⅝ yard of red-and-white check for binding

5⅜ yards of fabric for backing

71" x 95" piece of batting

Template plastic *or optional* 8" Easy Dresden ruler, by Darlene Zimmerman for EZ Quilting

CUTTING

The pattern for the large Dresden wedge is on page 22. Trace the pattern onto template plastic and cut it out, or use the optional Easy Dresden ruler.

From the white solid, cut:
1 rectangle, 30½" x 39½"
1 rectangle, 24" x 30½"
1 rectangle, 39½" x 40½"
1 rectangle, 24" x 40½"
3 strips, 8" x 42"; crosscut into 40 Dresden wedges*
4 strips, 2½" x 42"
6 squares, 8" x 8"; cut each square in half diagonally to yield 12 triangles.
2 rectangles, 2½" x 17"**
2 rectangles, 5¼" x 17"**

To use the fabric efficiently, alternately position the wide end of the wedge up and down.

**Cut these pieces after assembling the pinwheel blocks; see step 1 of "Piecing the Quilt Top" on page 21.*

From color 1, cut:
2 strips, 2" x 42"

From color 2, cut:
2 strips, 2½" x 42"

From color 3, cut:
2 strips, 2" x 42"

From color 4, cut:
2 strips, 1½" x 42"

From color 5, cut:
2 strips, 2" x 42"

From color 6, cut:
2 strips, 2½" x 42"

From color 7, cut:
2 strips, 2" x 42"

From color 8, cut:
2 strips, 1½" x 42"

From the black polka dot, cut:
3 squares, 5" x 5"

From the red-and-white check, cut:
8 strips, 2½" x 42"

MAKING THE PINWHEELS

This method yields enough wedges to make four pinwheels, two from each set of colors, but the quilt top includes only three. Use the extra wedges on the quilt back or to make a matching decorative pillow.

1. Sew one strip each of colors 1, 2, 3, and 4 and one white 2½" x 42" strip together in any order, with the white strip on one edge of the strip set. Press the seam allowances in one direction. Make two identical strip sets.

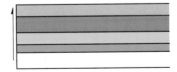

Make 2 strip sets.

2. Repeat step 1 to make two identical strip sets with colors 5, 6, 7, 8, and white (2½" x 42"), again placing the white strip on one edge of the strip set. Press the seam allowances in one direction.

3. Cut 20 Dresden wedges from the strip sets created in step 1, alternating the position of the wide end of the template from the white side of

the strip set to the colored side to make two sets of 10 matching wedges. Repeat to cut 20 wedges from the strip sets created in step 2, for a total of 40 wedges in four sets of 10. Sort the wedges into matching sets.

4. Arrange one set of colored wedges alternating with 10 white wedges and sew them together to make a complete circle. Press all the seam allowances in one direction around the circle. Make three, reserving the fourth set of wedges for another project or the back of the quilt.

FINISHING THE PINWHEELS

1. Lay one pinwheel on your cutting mat, centering the topmost wedge on a vertical cutting-mat line as shown. Position the raw edge of the topmost wedge above one of the mat's horizontal lines, with the line passing through the adjacent wedges on both sides of the central wedge. Smooth the fabric into place so that the circle of wedges is flat and without distortion.

Center.

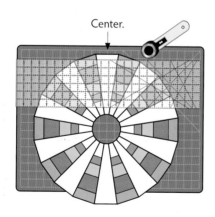

2. Lay an acrylic ruler along the horizontal line and use a rotary cutter to trim the circle, creating the first flat side of an octagon.

3. Rotate the pinwheel circle counterclockwise to place the next three wedges at the top of the pinwheel, and repeat the vertical and horizontal alignment as described in step 1. Trim as before.

4. Continue rotating the pinwheel and repeating steps 1 and 2 until you have made a total of eight cuts and turned the circle into an octagon. Make three octagons.

Pattern Up

If this freewheeling way of cutting your octagons bothers you, make an octagon template using the pattern on page 23. Trace the pattern onto cardboard or template plastic, rotating and repeating it to make a complete circle. Center the template on the pieced circle, trace the template edges, and cut out the octagon with scissors or a rotary cutter.

5. To turn the octagon into a square block, sew a white 8" triangle to each angled side of one octagon, right sides together. Press the seam allowances toward the white triangles. Repeat with the other two octagons.

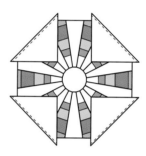

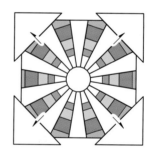

6. Trim each pinwheel block to measure 17" x 17". Since the Dresden wedges that make up each pinwheel shape have bias edges, they are easily pulled out of shape; squaring the blocks repairs any distortion. Your blocks may be larger or smaller than 17", but don't despair. Each pinwheel is pieced into a solid field of white, and any discrepancy can be eliminated by adding more or less white fabric when assembling the quilt top; the yardage includes an allowance for these adjustments.

7. Using the circle pattern on page 22, cut three circles from the black 5" squares. Center one black circle over the opening at the center of each pinwheel block and appliqué as desired referring to "Adaptable Appliqué," on page 21 for pointers.

PIECING THE QUILT TOP

1. If your pinwheel blocks didn't measure 17" square, adjust the size of the two white 2½" x 17" rectangles and two white 5¼" x 17" rectangles to yield a 63"-long row when the rectangles and blocks are assembled. Sew the 2½" x 17" rectangles between the three pinwheel blocks as shown. Sew the 5¼" x 17" rectangles to the ends of the pinwheel row. Press the seam allowances toward the white fabric.

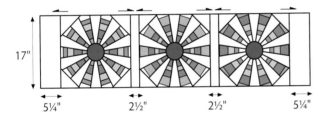

17"

5¼"   2½"   2½"   5¼"

2. Sew the 24" x 30½" white rectangle to one side of the 30½" x 39½" white rectangle to make a 30½" x 63" piece. Press the seam allowances open. Sew the assembled piece to the bottom of the pinwheel row. Press the seam allowances toward the white fabric.

Anyone Can Be Inspired

When I was thinking about new ways to use Dresdens, I wanted a way to make a Dresden Plate without the need to appliqué it onto a background fabric. The idea of a giant pinwheel came to me and this quilt was born. But just to show that anyone (even *you!*) can have her own inspi-rations, take a look a lovely quilt made by Geta Grama. It looks like a similar inspiration hit her. You can find her quilt at cadouri-din-inima.blogspot.ro/2011/11/dresden-quilt-finished.html

3. Sew the 24" x 40½" white rectangle to one side of the 39½" x 40½" white rectangle to make a 40½" x 63" piece. Press the seam allowances open. Sew the assembled piece to the top of the pinwheel row. Press the seam allowances toward the white fabric.

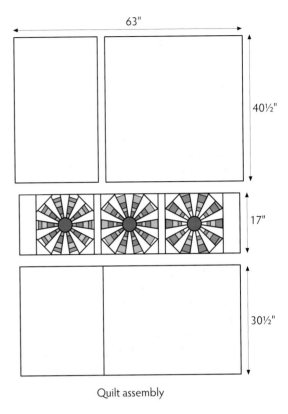

63"

40½"

17"

30½"

Quilt assembly

FINISHING THE QUILT

1. Cut the backing fabric in half to create two 96"-long pieces. Remove the selvages and sew the pieces together side by side. Press the seam allowances open.

2. Layer the backing, batting, and quilt top. Refer to "Basting" on page 61 and baste the layers together.

3. Quilt as desired. In the sample, densely quilted wavy lines suggest wind blowing through the pinwheels and give great movement to the quilt top. Trim the batting and backing to match the quilt top.

4. Referring to "Binding" on page 62, use the red-and-white checked strips to bind the quilt.

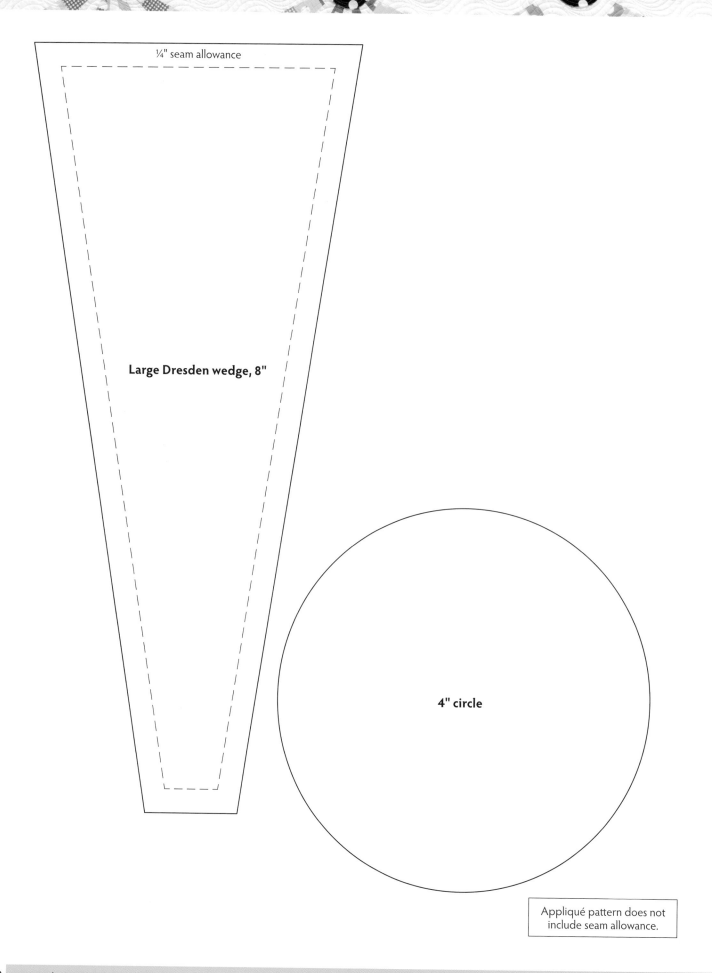

¼" seam allowance

Large Dresden wedge, 8"

4" circle

Appliqué pattern does not
include seam allowance.

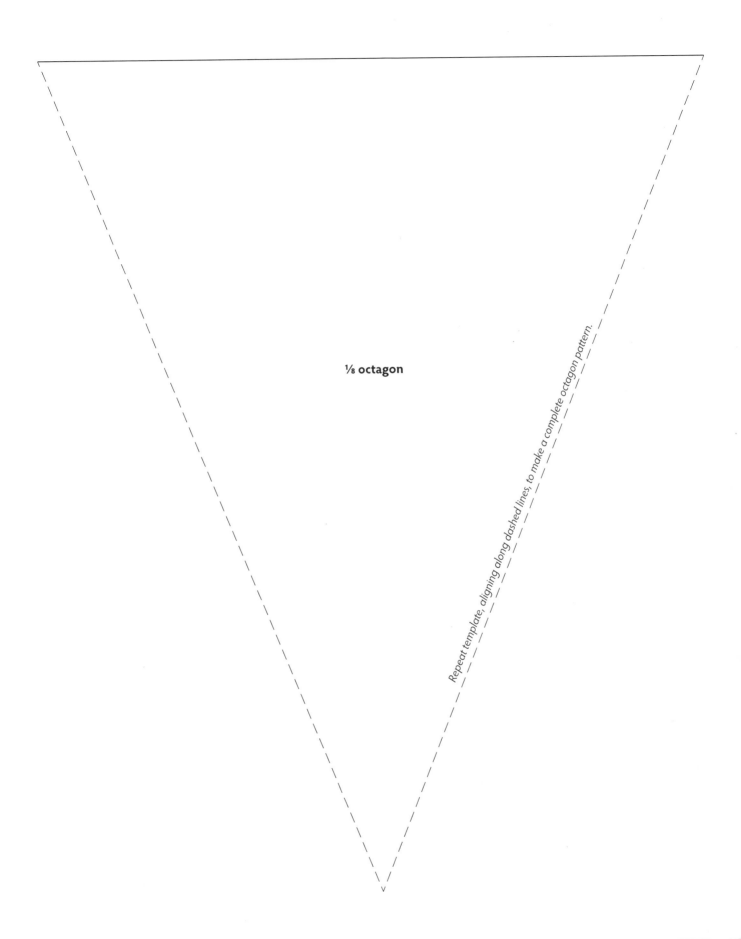

⅛ octagon

Repeat template, aligning along dashed lines, to make a complete octagon pattern.

zip it!

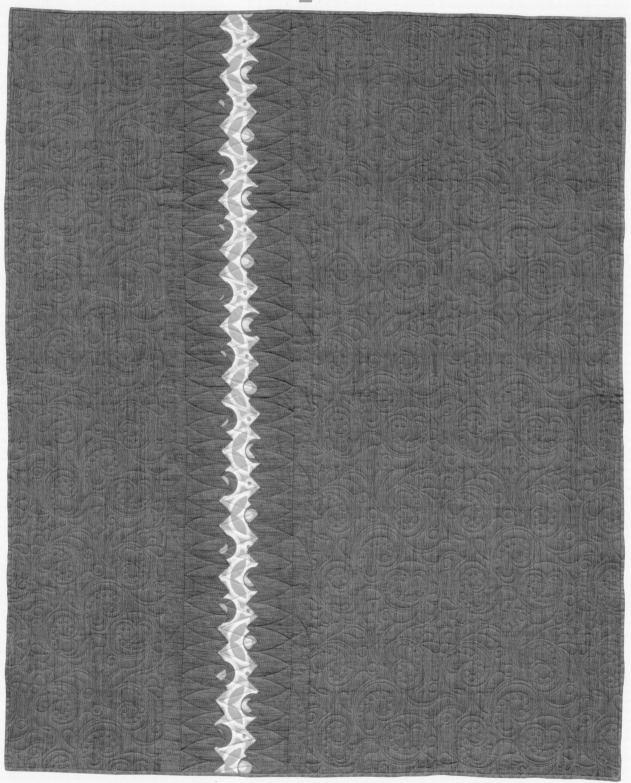

Designed by Dana Bolyard; pieced by Dolores Goodsend; machine quilted by Russ Adams
Finished quilt: 50" x 61"

*T*he online quilting community is a treasure trove of daily inspiration. Social media sites such as Flickr, Twitter, Pinterest, and Instagram are full of quilters sharing photos of what they're making. This quilt design is a direct result of such inspiration. My friend Dolores Goodsend shared a photo of a pillow she made that looked to me like a row of little houses lined up next to each other. I couldn't get that image out of my head, but in my mind I kept turning the little houses into teeth on a zipper. Thanks for the inspiration, Dolores, and for the superb piecing!

MATERIALS

Yardage is based on 42"-wide fabric.

2¾ yards of dark-gray fabric for background and zipper teeth

⅞ yard of bright print for zipper

½ yard of dark-pink print for binding

3⅞ yards of fabric for backing

58" x 69" piece of batting

CUTTING

From the dark-gray fabric, cut:

4 strips, 6" x 42"; crosscut into 62 rectangles, 2½" x 6"

3 strips, 2½" x 42"

Reserve the remaining fabric for the quilt background.

From the bright print, cut:

2 strips, 12½" x 42"

If you're using a large-scale print that you don't want to piece, purchase 1¾ yards of fabric and cut one strip, 12½" x 60", along the lengthwise *grain.*

From the dark-pink print, cut:

6 strips, 2½" x 42"

MAKING THE ZIPPER

Each 2½" x 6" rectangle will become a sort of Dresden wedge, with a pointed tip like many Dresden wedges, but with straight, rectangular sides rather than a wedge shape.

1. Fold a 2½" x 6" gray rectangle lengthwise with right sides together. Sew using a ¼" seam allowance across one short end. Trim the seam allowances diagonally at the folded edge to reduce bulk.

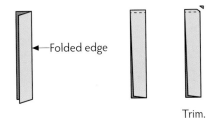

Folded edge

Trim.

2. Turn the point right side out and press the shape flat, centering the seam on the rectangle. Make 62.

Make 62.

3. Sew 31 units from step 2 together side by side to make one side of the zipper. Backstitch each seam at the end near the point. Press the seam allowances open. Trim any loose threads, especially at the zipper points. Make two.

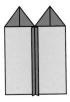

4. Sew the two 12½" x 42" bright-print strips together end to end. Press the seam allowances open and trim the fabric to measure 12½" x 61".

5. Lay one unit from step 3 along the left edge of the bright-print panel as shown, matching the long raw edges. The seam allowance at the bottom of the zipper-teeth strip will extend beyond the print panel, and one tooth point will align with the upper raw edge.

6. Position the second unit from step 3 on the print panel as shown, matching the long raw edges and aligning the valleys between points with the points of the left-hand zipper-teeth strip so that the two sets of teeth are offset.

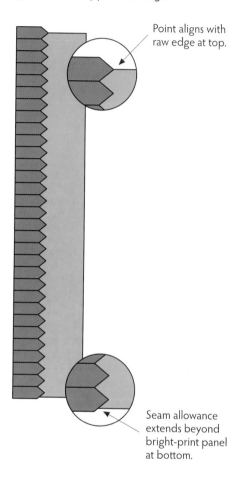

Point aligns with raw edge at top.

Seam allowance extends beyond bright-print panel at bottom.

7. Pin each set of zipper teeth securely to the print panel. Edgestitch ⅛" from the pointed edge of each zipper-teeth unit. Trim the excess gray fabric from the top and bottom of the assembled panel.

8. Sew the three 2½" x 42" gray strips together end to end and press the seam allowances open. Cut two lengths, 2½" x 61", from the pieced strip. Press ¼" to the wrong side along one long edge of each 61"-long strip.

9. Pin a unit from step 8 along each side of the zipper panel, matching the raw edges. Edgestitch ⅛" from the pressed edges.

Pressed edges

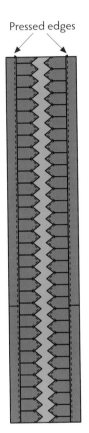

ASSEMBLING THE QUILT TOP

1. From the remaining dark-gray fabric, cut a piece 61" long. Divide this piece of fabric in two along its length, about 14" from the left edge. This creates the opening for the zipper panel. Its location may vary, but for the best visual appeal it should not be centered.

2. Pin the left edge of the zipper panel to the smaller of the two background sections with right sides together. Sew the zipper panel to the background piece and press the seam allowances toward the background. Repeat to attach the larger background rectangle to the right edge of the zipper panel.

3. Trim the completed quilt top to 50" x 61".

FINISHING THE QUILT

1. Cut the backing fabric in half to create two 69"-long pieces. Remove the selvages and sew the pieces together side by side. Press the seam allowances open.

2. Layer the backing, batting, and quilt top. Refer to "Basting" on page 61 and baste the layers together.

3. Quilt as desired. I used a pattern of zigzags along the zipper to echo and highlight it, guaranteeing it's the star of the show. The rest of the quilt features a flowing overall pattern. Trim the backing and batting to match the quilt top.

4. Referring to "Binding" on page 62, use the dark-pink strips to bind the quilt.

princess crowns

Designed and pieced by Dana Bolyard; machine quilted by Russ Adams
Finished quilt: 30½" x 30½"   •   **Finished block:** 7½" x 7½"

*J*ust because you have the mad skills to make Dresden Plates doesn't mean you have to. What about using those skills in a new way? What about making a less-than-full circle? And how about combining different sizes of Dresden wedges in the same block?

MATERIALS

Yardage is based on 42"-wide fabric.

1 yard of white solid for block backgrounds

1 fat eighth *each* of 16 assorted prints for crowns

⅓ yard of red dot for binding

1⅛ yards of fabric for backing

38" x 38" piece of batting

Template plastic *or optional* 8" Easy Dresden ruler, by Darlene Zimmerman for EZ Quilting

Sparkle Plenty

Fabrics with some glitter or sheen are perfect for these crowns.

CUTTING

The pattern for the 8" Dresden wedge is on page 22 of the "Three Wheeling" instructions; the 5" and 6" Dresden wedge patterns are on page 31. Trace the patterns onto template plastic and cut them out, or use the optional Easy Dresden ruler.

From the white solid, cut:

16 squares, 8½" x 8½"

From *each* print fat eighth, cut:

1 strip, 8" x 18"; crosscut into:
    1 large (8") Dresden wedge (16 total)
    2 medium (6") Dresden wedges (32 total)
    2 small (5") Dresden wedges (32 total)

From the red dot, cut:

4 strips, 2½" x 42"

PIECING THE BLOCKS

1. Fold one Dresden wedge in half lengthwise with right sides together. Sew across the wide end using a ¼" seam allowance. Trim the seam allowances diagonally at the folded edge to reduce bulk.

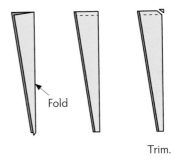

Fold

Trim.

2. Turn the pointed end of the wedge right side out. Press, centering the seam on the wedge. Make 80 wedges (16 large, 32 medium, and 32 small).

3. For the first block, select one 8" wedge, two matching 6" wedges, and two matching 5" wedges. Arrange these to form a crown as shown.

4. Working from left to right, place the first two wedges with right sides together, aligning the bottom edges, and pin. Stitch, backstitching at the upper (folded) edge to secure the seam. Press

the seam allowances toward the center of the crown, continuing to press the seam allowances of the longer wedge all the way to the top.

5. Sew the remaining wedges together. Press all the seam allowances toward the center of the crown. Press ¼" to the wrong side on the outer edge of each 5" wedge.

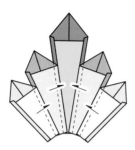

Pressing Pointers

I finger-press the wedge seam allowances as I sew them together, and then give the entire unit a thorough pressing with my iron after it's assembled. This makes the process a little easier and faster.

6. Use a rotary cutter and ruler to trim a small amount of fabric from the bottom of the crown, creating a straight edge perpendicular to the centerline of the longest wedge. Make 16 crowns of five wedges each.

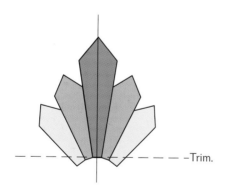

Make 16.

Royal Alignment

Center the middle wedge on a vertical cutting-mat line. Using the crosshatch marks on your ruler, position the ruler at right angles to the line on the mat, and then trim along the ruler's edge for a perfectly perpendicular cut that eliminates the curve at the bottom of the crown.

7. Pin the crown unit to an 8½" white square, centering the crown from side to side and aligning the raw edge of the crown with the bottom of the white square.

8. Edgestitch ⅛" from all the pressed edges of the crown, leaving the bottom edge unstitched. Trim the block to measure 8" x 8", keeping the crown centered from side to side. Make 16 blocks.

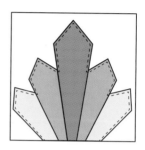

Make 16.

ASSEMBLING THE QUILT TOP

1. Arrange the blocks in four rows of four blocks each. Sew the blocks together into rows, and press the seam allowances in alternate directions from row to row.

2. Pin and sew the rows together to complete the quilt top. Press the seam allowances in one direction.

Quilt assembly

FINISHING THE QUILT

1. Layer the backing, batting, and quilt top. Refer to "Basting" on page 61 and baste the layers together.

2. Quilt as desired. This quilt's size makes it perfect for a wall hanging, so the quilting can be as intricate or as simple as you like. Embellishing the crowns with sparkly buttons or rhinestone gems would be a bit of extra fun. Trim the backing and batting to match the quilt top when the quilting and embellishing are complete.

3. Referring to "Binding" on page 62, use the red-dot strips to bind the quilt.

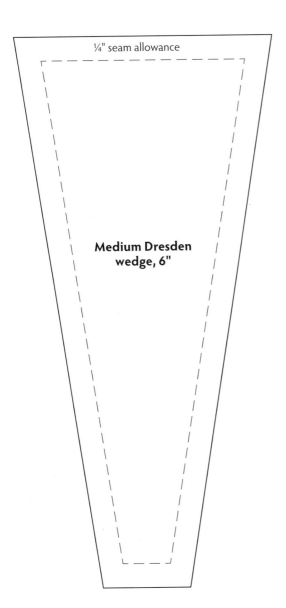

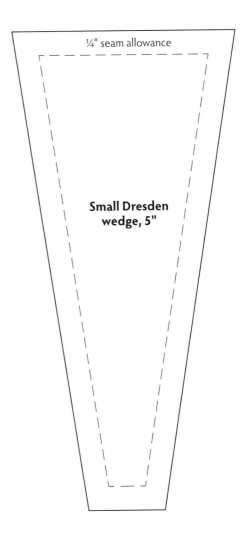

look around

Inspiration is everywhere, from the ground beneath your toe-tapping feet to the symbols on your computer keyboard. Color, texture, and design abound, just begging to be noticed. Grab a pencil and some graph paper and take a look around!

dance floor

Designed and pieced by Dana Bolyard; machine quilted by Russ Adams
Finished quilt: 65" x 65" • **Finished block:** 4½" x 4½"

*I*magine a formal wedding in the deep, deep South, with dapper clothes, mint juleps, parasols, and jazz bands. When I saw such a scene in a movie, the black-and-white dance floor just begged to be made into a quilt.

MATERIALS

Yardage is based on 42"-wide fabric.

3 yards of white solid for blocks and setting triangles

1 yard of black solid for blocks

⅝ yard of lime-green solid for binding

4 yards of fabric for backing

72" x 72" piece of batting

CUTTING

From the white solid, cut:

50 squares, 5" x 5"

2 squares, 35" x 35"; cut each square in half diagonally to yield 4 triangles*

From the black solid, cut:

50 squares, 5" x 5"

From the lime-green solid, cut:

7 strips, 2½" x 42"

See "Going Long," below, for tips on accurately cutting the large squares in half.

Going Long

Cutting the 35" x 35" squares diagonally requires a large cutting space and a very long ruler. If you don't have a cutting mat large enough, you can go old school by drawing the diagonal with a ruler and pencil and cutting it with scissors. To accomplish a straight cut without using a ruler, neatly fold the cut square in half diagonally and press the crease. Unfold the fabric and use scissors or a rotary cutter to cut along the crease.

PIECING THE QUILT TOP

1. Arrange the black and white squares in 10 rows of 10 squares each, beginning with a black square at the upper-left corner and alternating the color placement.

2. Sew the squares together into rows, and press the seam allowances open.

No-Show Pressing

I don't normally press seam allowances open, but doing so in this quilt ensures that the black seam allowances don't show through the white on the front of the quilt.

3. Pin and sew the rows together to complete the quilt center. Press the seam allowances open.

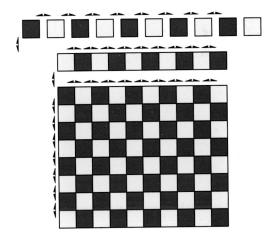

4. Fold one setting triangle in half and mark the center of the longest edge with a pin, taking care not to stretch the bias edge. The setting triangles are cut slightly larger than required, so you'll use the center point to help with proper positioning. Pin the long side of the triangle to one side of the black-and-white patchwork as shown, matching the centers and allowing the triangle points to

extend beyond the edges of the patchwork. Sew the seam and press the seam allowances toward the quilt center.

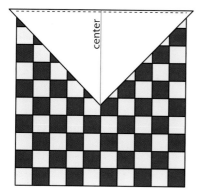

5. Repeat step 4 to sew a second setting triangle to the opposite side of the quilt center. Stitch the last two triangles to the remaining edges. Press the seam allowances toward the center.

6. Square up the quilt top to measure 65" x 65", keeping the pieced section centered. You'll be trimming about 1" outside the intersections of the setting-triangle seams.

FINISHING THE QUILT

1. Cut the backing fabric in half to create two 72"-long pieces. Remove the selvages and sew the pieces together side by side. Press the seam allowances open.

2. Layer the backing, batting, and quilt top. Refer to "Basting" on page 61 and baste the layers together.

3. Quilt as desired. A swirling, twirling quilting design seemed most appropriate for this dance floor. Trim the batting and backing to match the quilt top.

4. Referring to "Binding" on page 62, use the green strips to bind the quilt.

patchwork whale

Designed and pieced by Dana Bolyard; machine quilted by Russ Adams
Finished quilt: 63½" x 87½"

I'm particularly fond of whales. What are you particularly fond of? Can you sketch it on graph paper and turn it into a quilt?

MATERIALS

Yardage is based on 42"-wide fabric.

1⅞ yards of yellow solid for background

1⅞ yards of light-blue solid for background

1⅓ yards *total* of assorted blue prints for whale

1¼ yards of light-gray solid for background

⅜ yards *total* of white tone-on-tone prints for whale

3" x 3" square of black solid for whale's eye

⅔ yard for blue stripe for binding

5⅓ yards of fabric for backing

71" x 95" piece of batting

Got the Blues?

Using a wide variety of blue hues and prints will add interest, texture, and movement to your whale; you'll need over a hundred 3" squares, plus more than a dozen 3⅞" squares, of blue. This is an excellent time to raid your scrap bin in search of blue! Just keep in mind that you want all of the fabrics to read as blue.

CUTTING

From the white tone-on-tone prints, cut:
20 squares, 3" x 3"
5 squares, 3⅜" x 3⅜"

From the light-gray solid, cut:
1 rectangle, 10½" x 8" (A)
1 rectangle, 5½" x 30½" (B)
1 rectangle, 3" x 15½" (C)
1 square, 15½" x 15½" (D)
1 rectangle, 3" x 30½" (E)
2 strips, 2" x 30½"
11 squares, 3⅜" x 3⅜"
37 squares, 3" x 3"

From the assorted blue prints, cut:
115 squares, 3" x 3"
14 squares, 3⅜" x 3⅜"

From the yellow solid, cut:
1 rectangle, 27½" x 63½"

From the light-blue solid, cut:
1 rectangle, 30½" x 63½"

From the blue stripe, cut:
8 strips, 2½" x 42"

PIECING THE WHALE

The whale is really the star of this show. It's constructed like a mosaic from 3" squares and half-square-triangle units.

1. Draw a diagonal line from corner to corner on the wrong side of each 3⅜" white square.

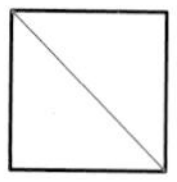

2. With right sides together, pin a marked white square to a 3⅜" gray square. Sew ¼" from both sides of the drawn line.

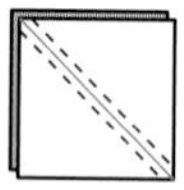

3. Cut along the drawn diagonal line to create two half-square-triangle units, each 3" x 3". Press the seam allowances toward the gray fabric and trim the "wings."

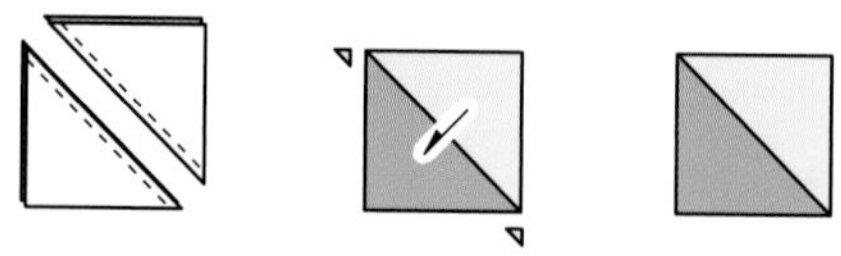

Make 2.

4. Draw a diagonal line from corner to corner on the wrong side of each remaining 3⅜" gray square. With right sides together, pin each marked gray square to a 3⅜" blue square.

5. Repeat steps 2 and 3 to yield 20 gray/blue half-square-triangle units. You will need only 19 units; however, extra units give you added flexibility during the scrappy construction of the whale.

6. Use the four remaining marked 3⅜" white squares and four 3⅜" blue squares to make eight white/blue half-square-triangle units. You will use four and have four left over.

7. Work on the whale in quadrants, following the illustrations provided. For quadrant I, use 16 gray squares, 11 blue squares, and nine gray/blue half-square-triangle units to piece three rows, pressing the seam allowances in alternate directions from row to row. Join the three rows to make the top section, and press the seam allowances in one direction. Sew together five gray squares, 13 blue squares, and six gray/blue half-square-triangle units to make the bottom section, pressing as before. Sew gray rectangle A to the left edge of the bottom section and press the seam allowances toward A. Join the top and bottom sections to complete the quadrant.

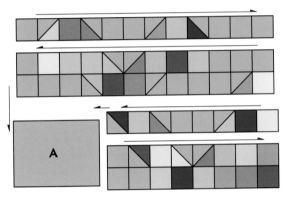

Quadrant I

8. For quadrant II, use 44 blue squares and four gray squares. Assemble them into rows, pressing the seam allowances in alternate directions from row to row. Sew the rows together and press the seam allowances in one direction. Add gray rectangle B to the top edge of the pieced unit and press the seam allowances toward B.

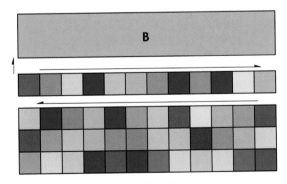

Quadrant II

9. For quadrant III, arrange 20 blue squares, six gray squares, and four gray/blue half-square-triangle units into five rows of six squares each. Sew the blocks into rows, pressing the seam allowances in alternate directions from row to row. Sew the rows together and press the seam allowances in one direction. Sew gray rectangle C to the bottom of the pieced unit and press the seam allowances toward C. Stitch gray square D to the left edge of the unit and press the seam allowances toward D.

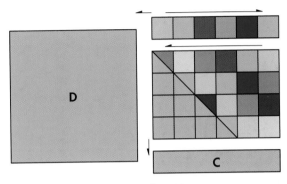

Quadrant III

10. For quadrant IV, assemble the remaining blue, white, gray, and black squares and half-square-triangle units as shown and press as above. Sew gray rectangle E to the bottom of the pieced unit and press the seam allowances toward E.

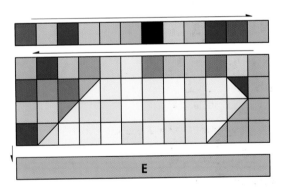

Quadrant IV

11. Pin and sew quadrant I to quadrant II and press the seam allowances toward quadrant II. Pin and sew quadrants III and IV together and press the seam allowances toward quadrant III, as shown on page 40.

12. Pin and sew the sections of the whale panel together and press the seam allowances in one direction. Sew a 2" x 30½" gray rectangle to each side of the pieced whale panel. Press the seam allowances toward the gray rectangles.

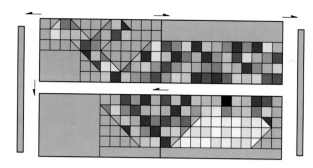

ASSEMBLING THE QUILT TOP

1. Pin and sew the light-blue rectangle to the top edge of the completed whale panel. Press the seam allowances toward the blue rectangle.

2. Pin and sew the yellow rectangle to the top edge of the light-blue rectangle. Press the seam allowances toward the blue rectangle.

FINISHING THE QUILT

1. Cut the backing fabric in half to create two 96"-long pieces. Remove the selvages and sew the pieces together side by side. Press the seam allowances open. Trim to 71" x 95" if desired.

2. Layer the backing, batting, and quilt top. Refer to "Basting" on page 61 and baste the layers together.

3. Quilt as desired. I chose a wavy pattern suggestive of the ocean, its bubbles, and even octopus tentacles. Trim the batting and backing to match the quilt top.

4. Referring to "Binding" on page 62, use the blue-striped strips to bind the quilt.

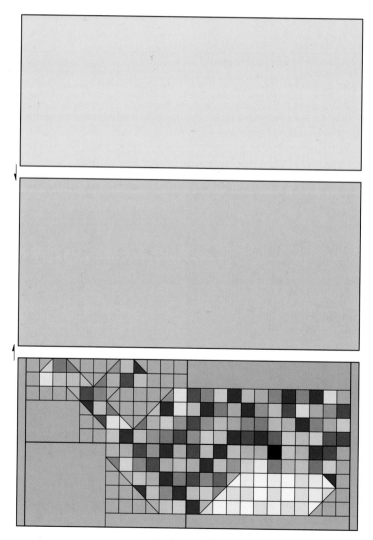

Quilt assembly

ampersand

Designed and pieced by Dana Bolyard; machine quilted by Russ Adams
Finished quilt: 63½" x 68"

*O*ur modern world is full of graphic textual symbols. The ampersand strikes my fancy. What strikes yours: the # sign, the @ symbol, or . . . ? Make an ampersand quilt, or use this pattern as a springboard for turning your own favorite symbol into a quilt.

MATERIALS

Yardage is based on 42"-wide fabric.

3¼ yards of navy solid for background

⅞ yard *total* of assorted bright solids for ampersand

⅝ yard of bright-pink solid for binding

4 yards of fabric for backing

71" x 75½" piece of batting

Less than Scrappy

If your stash doesn't include many solid scraps, purchase either seven fat quarters *or* nine fat eighths to use instead. Cut five squares, 5" x 5", from *each* of the fat quarters, *or* four squares, 5" x 5", from *each* of the fat eighths. You'll have a few left over, but the extras allow flexibility when arranging the colors.

CUTTING

From the navy solid, cut:
1 rectangle, 27½" x 32"
135 squares, 5" x 5"

From the bright solids, cut:
33 squares, 5" x 5"

From the bright pink, cut:
7 strips, 2½" x 42"

PIECING THE QUILT TOP

This quilt is constructed in quadrants for easier handling. As you assemble the rows within each quadrant, press the seam allowances in alternate directions from row to row.

1. Using the 5" squares of navy and assorted brights, assemble quadrants I, III, and IV as shown above right. Within each quadrant, sew the squares into rows and then join the rows to complete the

quadrant. Quadrant II consists simply of the 27½" x 32" navy rectangle.

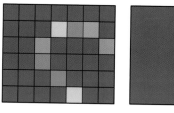

Quadrant I   Quadrant II

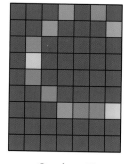 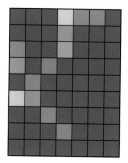

Quadrant III   Quadrant IV

2. Pin and sew quadrants I and II together. Press the seam allowances toward quadrant II. Sew quadrant III to quadrant IV and press the seam allowances toward quadrant III.

3. Pin and sew the two sections together and press the seam allowances in one direction.

FINISHING THE QUILT

1. Cut the backing fabric in half to create two 72"-long pieces. Remove the selvages and sew the pieces together side by side. Press the seam allowances open.

2. Layer the backing, batting, and quilt top. Refer to "Basting" on page 61 and baste the layers together.

3. Quilt as desired. This quilt begged me for more ampersands in the quilting so they were stitched in the bright squares. Trim the backing and batting to match the quilt top.

4. Referring to "Binding" on page 62, use the bright-pink strips to bind the quilt.

Surrounded By Inspiration

Pictured here are some things that have inspired me. Some appear in quilts I've made, and others are on my list of "must-makes" for the future.

The hashtag from social media and other punctuation marks

Rainbow colors of canvas footwear

Amusement park rides and their colorful details

Veggies and fruits in their natural environments

break the rules

My mother-in-law first introduced me to quilting years ago. From cutting and piecing to pressing and binding, she taught me the skills that I use each and every day. She taught me how to do them well. She instilled in me the expertise to choose quality fabric, stitch secure seams, and bind a quilt to ensure strength and durability.

But one thing I know for sure is that there are no rules in quilting. And if you think there are, then it's time you try breaking a few.

scribble

Designed, pieced, and quilted by Dana Bolyard
Finished quilt: 48½" x 48½" • **Finished block:** 3" x 3"

*R emember when you were little and were
told not to scribble? I'm officially giving
you permission to scribble—with your quilting!*

MATERIALS

Yardage is based on 42"-wide fabric.

1⅝ yards of teal solid for blocks

½ yard *each* of pink, cheddar, and yellow solids for blocks

½ yard *total* of assorted black prints for blocks

3⅜ yards of black print for binding and backing*

56" x 56" piece of batting*

*Because this is intended as a quilt-it-yourself project, you may not want to allow the full 4" needed by a long-arm quilter on all sides of the quilt backing and batting, but you should allow at least 2" on each side to accommodate shrinkage during quilting. After cutting the backing fabric, you'll have a rectangle of fabric left over that can be cut into 2½"-wide strips for binding the quilt. If you prefer to use a separate fabric for binding, purchase ½ yard and cut six strips, 2½" x 42".

Triangle Variety

I selected 12 black-print squares from a collection of black-and-white prints, purchased as a pack of precut 10" squares.

CUTTING

From the teal solid, cut:
128 squares, 4" x 4"

From *each* of the pink, cheddar, and yellow solids, cut:
32 squares, 4" x 4" (96 total)

From the assorted black prints, cut:
32 squares, 4" x 4"

From the black print for binding and backing, cut on the *lengthwise grain*:
2 pieces, 42" x 56"; from 1 piece, cut 4 strips, 2½" x 56"

PIECING THE BLOCKS

1. Draw a diagonal line from corner to corner on the wrong side of each teal square.

2. With right sides together, pin each teal square to a pink, cheddar, yellow, or black square. Sew ¼" from both sides of the drawn diagonal line. Cut along the diagonal line.

3. Press the seam allowances open. Trim and square up the half-square-triangle units to measure 3½" x 3½". Make 256 blocks.

Make 256.

Flat to Flatter

I don't usually press seam allowances open, but doing so in this quilt makes matching the seams easier and reduces bulk. It takes a little more time at this stage of the process, but when you start quilting, you'll be glad you did it!

ASSEMBLING THE QUILT TOP

1. Arrange the blocks in 16 rows of 16 blocks each, orienting the diagonal seams in the same direction throughout the quilt. Move the blocks around until you are pleased with the color placement; you may prefer to have a concentration of pinks, cheddars, yellows, or blacks in a certain area.

2. Pin and sew the blocks together into rows, and press the seam allowances in alternate directions from row to row. If you prefer, you may assemble the quilt top in four sections, each containing eight rows of eight blocks.

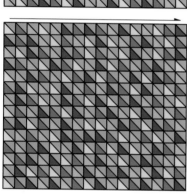

Quilt assembly

Optional quilt assembly

3. Sew the rows (or quadrants) together to complete the quilt top. Press the seam allowances in one direction.

FINISHING THE QUILT

1. Sew the two large backing pieces together side by side and press the seam allowances open.

2. Layer the backing, batting, and quilt top. Refer to "Basting" on page 61 and baste the layers together.

3. Free-motion quilt with a scribbling motion. You may want to practice on a quilt sandwich made from scraps of fabric and batting to decide how densely to quilt and how long to make each scribbled line before switching directions. Have fun and get comfortable with the quilting motion. Remember, you have permission to scribble any way you want!

Free-motion quilting gives the quilt "Scribble" its name.

4. Trim the backing and batting to match the quilt top.

5. Referring to "Binding" on page 62, use the 2½"-wide black-print strips to bind the quilt.

kite strings

Designed and pieced by Dana Bolyard; machine quilted by Russ Adams and Dana Bolyard
Finished quilt: 51½" x 55½"

*C*onventional wisdom tells us that once you send your quilt to a long-arm quilter, all you have left to do is add the binding and you're done. But that rule can be broken, too. Part of my plan for "Kite Strings" all along was to add my own quilting when the long-arm quilter was finished. I wanted the string connecting the kite ties to be quilted, becoming an integral part of the design.

MATERIALS

Yardage is based on 42"-wide fabric.

10 fat eighths of assorted warm solids, in graduated hues from dark red to light yellow, for kite tails

3⅜ yards of aqua solid for background

½ yard of green solid for binding

3½ yards of fabric for backing

60" x 63" piece of batting

Copy paper

CUTTING

From *each* assorted fat eighth, cut:

2 squares, 4" x 4" (20 total)

From the aqua solid, cut:

20 rectangles, 4" x 6½"

10 rectangles, 3½" x 8"

20 rectangles, 3½" x 6½"

10 rectangles, 3½" x 7"

12 strips, 5½" x 41"

From the green solid, cut:

6 strips, 2½" x 42"

PIECING THE KITE TAILS

The 10 kite tails are created with foundation piecing. Basic instructions for the technique are included below; you can find more information, free, at ShopMartingale.com/HowtoQuilt. Accurate cutting and grain-line placement aren't as important in foundation piecing as they are in other techniques; we've precut rectangles for each foundation area for ease of handling.

Waste Not

Foundation piecing produces stunningly accurate results but can be a fabric waster. Although it's not essential, cutting rectangles and squares of approximately the size needed for the foundation-pieced block reduces the waste.

1. Make 10 copies *each* of foundation patterns A and B on pages 53 and 54. For each kite tail, you'll use one warm color from the fat eighths; work on the matching A and B blocks at the same time to avoid confusion.

2. Position a 4" x 6½" aqua rectangle on foundation A, covering the area marked A1. The wrong side of the fabric should lie against the unprinted side of the foundation; holding it up to a sunny window or bright light will help you see the fabric placement. Be sure the fabric extends at least ¼" beyond the printed seam lines framing area A1. Pin the fabric to the foundation, or use a dot of basting glue to hold it in place.

3. Lay a 4" square of warm-hued fabric on the aqua rectangle, right sides together. Position the square with its raw edge at least ¼" beyond the seam line between areas A1 and A2. Flip it over to confirm that it will cover area A2 after it's been sewn and pressed into position, and then return it to its sewing position. With the printed side of the foundation on top, sew along the line between areas A1 and A2, beginning and ending at least ¼" beyond the ends of the line. Use a shortened machine stitch (1.5 mm) to make removing the foundation easier.

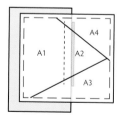

4. Smooth the square of fabric into place, folding it along the seam line, to check that it covers area A2 completely; adjust and sew again if necessary. When the positioning is correct, trim the seam allowances to ¼". Do not cut the foundation paper. Press the colored square into place, pinning if necessary.

5. Lay a 3½" x 8" aqua rectangle on the previous fabrics, right sides together, checking its placement to cover area A3 and allowing at least ¼" for the seam. Sew, trim, and press as before.

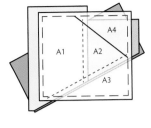 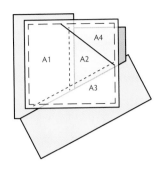

6. Position and stitch a 3½" x 6½" aqua rectangle to cover area A4. Trim the seam allowance to ¼", then press the entire block. Stitch around the edges of the block just outside the stitching line. Use a rotary cutter and ruler to trim the block along the cutting line, making a 5½" x 6" block. Don't remove the foundation paper yet.

7. Assemble a B block in the same way, using a 4" x 6½" aqua rectangle for B1; a 4" colored square for B2; a 3½" x 6½" aqua rectangle for B3; and a 3½" x 7" aqua rectangle for B4.

8. Make 10 pairs of A and B blocks, one pair using each warm hue.

9. Pin and sew matching A and B blocks together to yield a 5½" x 11½" kite tail, aligning the stitching lines printed on the foundations. Make 10.

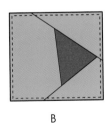 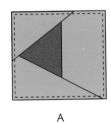

B   A

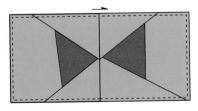

Make 10.

PIECING THE QUILT TOP

1. The kite tails progress across the quilt top, from the darkest red at the upper left to the lightest yellow at the lower right. Each row of the quilt is assembled from a paper-pieced unit and one 5½" x 41" aqua strip; cut eight of the strips into two pieces each, referring to the illustration below, and use full-width strips to assemble the top and bottom rows. Arrange the pieces as you wish them to appear in the quilt.

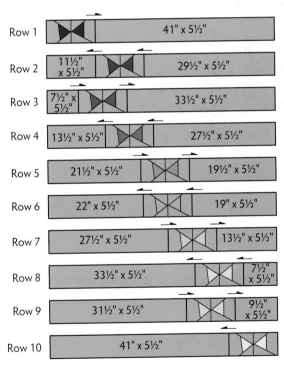

Quilt assembly.
Measurements are cut sizes.

2. Pin and sew the pieces in each row together, and press the seam allowances in one direction, alternating the direction from row to row. Carefully tear the foundation papers from the pieced blocks. Trim the aqua strips if necessary so each row measures 5½" x 51½".

3. Sew the rows together and press the seam allowances in one direction.

4. Sew the remaining two 5½" x 41" aqua strips together and press the seam allowances to one side. Cut the strip to measure 5½" x 51½".

5. Sew the strip from step 4 to the bottom of the quilt top and press the seam allowances to one side.

FINISHING THE QUILT

1. Cut the backing fabric in half to create two 60"-long pieces. Remove the selvages and sew the pieces together side by side. Press the seam allowances open.

2. Layer the backing, batting, and quilt top. Refer to "Basting" on page 61 and baste the layers together.

3. Quilt as desired. Swirls and dots in the quilting provide movement and the perfect windy effect for the flying kite strings. Trim the backing and batting to match the quilt top.

4. Thread your machine with black thread and use free-motion quilting to create the kite string connecting the colorful kite tails. Add some randomly placed loops to the kite string for extra interest.

5. Referring to "Binding" on page 62, use the green-solid strips to bind the quilt.

Add the kite string with black thread as the final quilting touch.

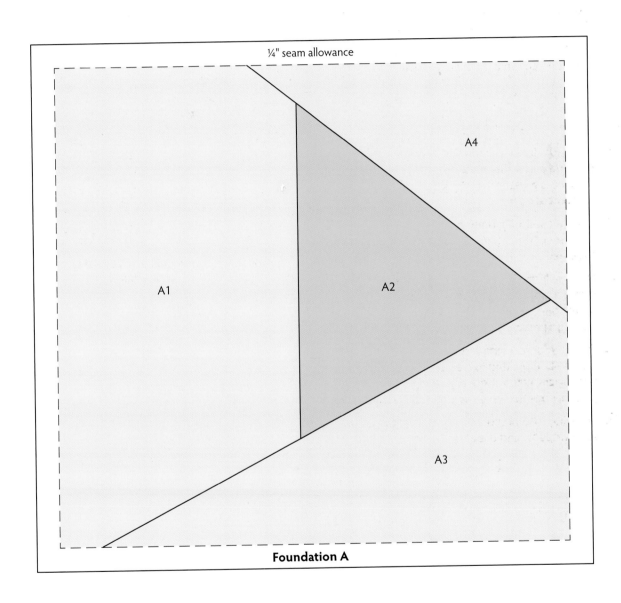

¼" seam allowance

A4

A1

A2

A3

Foundation A

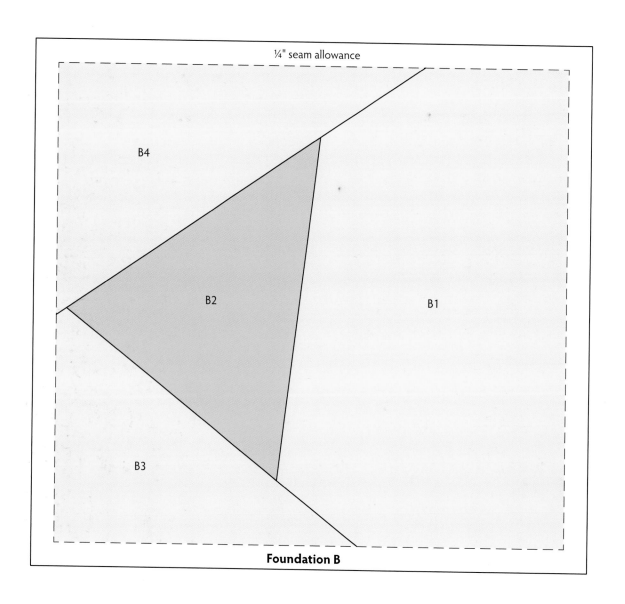

¼" seam allowance

B4

B2

B1

B3

Foundation B

posy patrol

Designed and pieced by Dana Bolyard; machine quilted by Russ Adams
Finished quilt: 63½" x 84½" • **Finished block:** 10½" x 10½"

*D*o you see popular trends within the quilting world without knowing what to do with them? When you come across a trend you like, make it your own! That's exactly how this quilt came about. My mother has a long-standing tradition of walking around her yard each day to see what's blooming, and lately I've been doing the same thing. We affectionately call this walk our daily posy patrol. In this quilt I took the popular approach of combining richly saturated prints and very pale (or "low-volume") fabrics, and I merged that trend with the notion of our daily walks.

MATERIALS

Yardage is based on 42"-wide fabric.

48 fat eighths of assorted bright prints for blocks*

39 fat eighths *or* 20 fat quarters of pale prints for blocks

¾ yard of multicolored polka dot for block centers

⅝ yard of black floral for binding

5¼ yards of fabric for backing

71" x 92" piece of batting

Template plastic

If you prefer to use scraps for the bright prints, you'll need four 4" x 4" squares each of 48 different prints.

CUTTING

Trace pattern pieces A and B on page 57 onto template plastic and cut them out.

From *each* of the bright prints, cut:
4 of pattern A (192 total)

From the pale prints, cut:
192 of pattern B
192 squares, 4" x 4"

From the multicolored polka dot, cut:
48 squares, 4" x 4"

From the black floral, cut:
8 strips, 2½" x 42"

Making It Easy

For easier cutting, cut a 4" square for each A and B piece (192 of each). Match the straight sides of the template to the raw edges of a square and mark the curved edge. Cut along the curve with scissors.

PIECING THE BLOCKS

1. Fold a bright A piece and a pale B piece in half to find the center of each curved edge. Pin the pieces with right sides together, matching the centers. Match and pin the pieces at each end of the curved edge. Continue to pin around the curve, easing the fabrics to fit.

2. Stitch around the curve. Press the seam allowances toward B, clipping the seam allowances as necessary.

3. Repeat steps 1 and 2 to make 192 units. Vary the placement of the B pieces so that no set of four matching A pieces uses the same pale print twice.

Beat the Curve

These curved units are similar to traditional Drunkard's Path blocks. Curves can be tricky and intimidating, but if you pin well and take your time, you can do it!

4. Arrange four units from step 3 that have matching bright prints, four assorted pale squares, and one polka-dot square to create a block. Sew the squares into rows and press the seam allowances toward the pale squares. Sew the rows together and press the seam allowances in one direction. Make 48 Posy blocks.

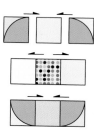

Make 48.

ASSEMBLING THE QUILT TOP

1. Arrange the blocks in eight rows of six blocks each. Sew the blocks together into rows, and press the seam allowances in alternate directions from row to row.

2. Sew the rows together and press the seam allowances in one direction.

FINISHING THE QUILT

1. Cut the backing fabric in half to create two 94"-long pieces. Remove the selvages and sew the pieces together side by side. Press the seam allowances open.

2. Layer the backing, batting, and quilt top. Refer to "Basting" on page 61 and baste the layers together.

3. Quilt as desired. I chose a spiral quilting design to emphasize the curves of each posy, but an allover floral motif would be pretty as well. Trim the backing and batting to match the quilt top.

4. Referring to "Binding" on page 62, use the black floral strips to bind the quilt.

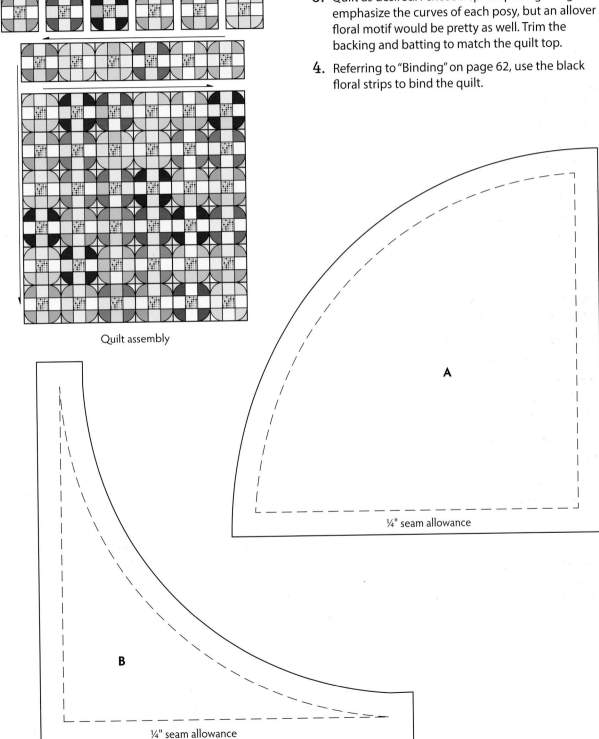

Quilt assembly

A

¼" seam allowance

B

¼" seam allowance

terms

Quiltmaking has its own vocabulary, and knowing the basic words and phrases is helpful.

Appliqué. A technique of sewing pieces of fabric on top of another piece of fabric to create designs or patterns. Appliqué can be done by hand or machine, or with fusible web.

Basting. A method of keeping layers—especially the quilt top, batting, and backing—together during later sewing or quilting. See "Basting" on page 61 for more information.

Batting. The layer between the quilt top and backing that gives thickness and warmth to a finished quilt. Batting can be cotton, wool, silk, bamboo, polyester, or a blend. I prefer 100% cotton batting for its weight and washability.

Bias. The diagonal direction across the surface of a woven fabric. While any direction not parallel to the grain is considered bias, the term usually refers to the true bias, at a 45° angle to the line of warp and weft. Fabric cut on the bias stretches easily and should be handled and sewn with care to avoid distortion.

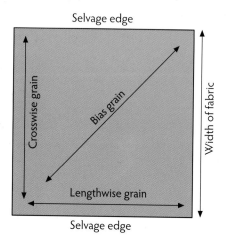

Binding. A strip of fabric sewn over the edges of the quilt layers to finish the raw edges. See "Binding" on page 62 for more information.

Border. A strip of fabric sewn around the perimeter of a quilt top, or a portion thereof, acting as a frame around the center of the quilt top.

Chain piecing. Feeding quilt pieces through the sewing machine one after another without snipping threads between pieces. Chain piecing saves both time and thread, and its repetitive nature often improves accuracy.

Directional print. Fabric with a printed pattern that has a definite direction or nap. Pay close attention to match the design's orientation or the nap when piecing.

Echo quilting. Quilting stitches placed next to a shape or block, following the outline of the shape or block and echoing its design.

Feed dogs. The teeth under the throat plate on a sewing machine that grab and move the fabric through the machine. The feed dogs are up and operational during regular sewing-machine operation and usually lowered for free-motion quilting.

Finger-pressing. Using your fingers to press a seam allowance instead of, or before, pressing with an iron.

Foundation paper piecing. A block-assembly method in which fabric pieces are sewn directly to a pattern printed on paper. This method takes the hassle out of cutting very precise and intricate fabric pieces and can result in incredibly detailed and accurate quilt-block construction.

Free-motion quilting. A style of machine quilting in which the quilter creates the design by moving the quilt under the needle and a darning foot. Because the feed dogs are usually lowered or covered, they don't move the fabric through the machine and the quilter is free to change directions at will.

Grain. The lengthwise and crosswise threads of a woven fabric (also referred to as the warp and weft).

Hand quilting. Sewing the three layers of a quilt together by hand, using a small needle and a running stitch.

Hanging sleeve. A tube of fabric the width of the quilt that is attached to the top of the quilt back, allowing the quilt to be hung on a wall for display.

Layout. The arrangement of the blocks, strips, pieces, or rows in a quilt top.

Long-arm quilting. Quilting that is done on a specialized long-bed quilting machine in conjunction with a frame.

On point. A square block that is set into a quilt on the diagonal, with its corners oriented at the top, bottom, and sides. The block may be appliquéd on point to other pieces or positioned on point in the quilt layout.

Quilt guild. An organization of quilters that provides opportunities to share projects, instructions, and community service. Check with your local quilt shop to find quilt guilds near you.

Sashing. Strips of fabric sewn between pieced blocks and/or block rows to separate them from others.

Scrap quilt. Any quilt made with fabric left over from other projects or salvaged from other goods such as clothing.

Template. A shape used for tracing, cutting, or sewing. Dozens of manufactured templates are available for purchase, or you can make your own from cardboard, template plastic, or freezer paper.

Tied quilt. A quilt in which knotted strings, rather than rows of quilting stitches, are used to hold the layers of the quilt together.

tools

*E*very quilter needs a few essential tools to get started, and other items make nice additions to growing quilting studios.

Sewing machine. Unless you plan to hand sew, a sewing machine is a must. A basic sewing machine with a straight stitch and a few other basic stitches, such as a zigzag, is really all you need. A machine that accommodates accessory sewing feet is beneficial so that you can use a walking foot, a ¼" foot, and a darning foot from time to time.

Needles. You'll need needles, both for your sewing machine and for finishing quilt bindings by hand. Needles come in a variety of sizes and types based on their function; in general, a smaller number means a smaller or finer sewing-machine needle, but the opposite is true for hand-sewing needles.

Sewing-machine needles with a sharp point (rather than a ball point) in sizes from 11 to 14 work well for most quiltmaking tasks. Consult your sewing machine's manual for more information about the proper needles for your machine.

When selecting needles for hand finishing your quilt, experiment with sizes until you find something comfortable for you. Balance the ease of passing a small needle through many fabric layers with the ease of threading a larger needle, and choose a needle that's large enough to protect the thread as you sew.

Scissors. Invest in a good pair of fabric scissors that you will use *only* for fabric. It's also handy to have a smaller pair at your work station for snipping stray threads.

Rotary cutter. These super-sharp rolling cutters work exactly like pizza cutters and make fast, accurate cutting a breeze. They can be dangerous, so operate with care. Always use with a rotary-cutting mat.

Rotary-cutting mat. Essential when cutting with a rotary cutter, this mat protects the surface you're cutting on and provides general measurement markers to use when cutting. They are available in many sizes, and I use my 24" x 36" cutting mat every time I sew.

Rotary-cutting rulers. These acrylic rulers work in conjunction with rotary cutters and mats to make cutting fabric quick and easy.

Iron and ironing board. Properly pressing fabric yardage and seam allowances is a big part of good quilting. The more you quilt, the more you'll appreciate a hot steam iron and large pressing space.

Thread. You must have thread if you plan to sew. I prefer a high-quality, 100% cotton thread made with long cotton fibers to reduce lint and add durability. Your user's manual may also offer thread recommendations for your sewing machine.

Straight pins. When piecing, you'll often use straight pins to hold sections together as you sew. I like to use 1½"-long straight pins.

Fabric pencils or marking pens. When a pattern or your own idea requires you to mark on fabric, be sure to use a marking tool designed for that use. Several options for fabric pencils and marking pens are readily available; choose one that either fades over time or disappears with washing. It's a good idea to test the pen or pencil on scrap fabric before using it to mark your quilt patches.

tips and tricks

The more you sew, the more you know. Here are some things I've learned that I'd like to pass along to you.

CHOOSING FABRIC

You want your quilt to stand the test of time, so construct it using quality fabrics. When selecting fabric, keep these pointers in mind:

- Fabric that is tightly woven is stronger and lasts longer.

- Your quilt will be washed countless times over its life span, so be sure the dyes are colorfast.

- The 100% cotton fabrics available at quilt shops are the best money can buy, and today's manufacturers create fabric designs to satisfy any aesthetic. Visit your local brick-and-mortar shops and remember that you can find amazing fabric shops online as well.

- Yardage requirements for projects in this book, as well as most patterns you can purchase, are based on fabric with 42" of usable width—that is, the width available after the selvages are removed.

- When I use quality quilting fabrics, I don't prewash my fabrics before sewing. If you're unsure of the manufacturer or origin of any fabric you plan to use, I recommend prewashing both to eliminate shrinkage and to test the colorfastness of dyes. This is especially true of vintage fabrics. If you prewash one fabric in a quilt or project, it's a good idea to prewash them all.

What's a Precut?

Precuts are just that—fabrics already cut for purchase. They may be cut by the fabric store or come bundled in coordinated groupings cut and packaged by the manufacturer. They offer an easy and more affordable way to purchase an entire line of fabric.

Fat quarter: an 18" x 21" cut

Fat eighth: a 9" x 21" or 11" x 18" cut

Moda Jelly Roll: a group of 2½" x 42" strips

Charm pack: a group of 5" x 5" squares

Moda Layer Cake: a group of 10" x 10" squares

Moda Honeycomb: a group of precut 6" hexagons

CUTTING FABRIC

1. Always start by squaring off the fabric edge; that is, make sure the cut end is perpendicular to the selvages. This ensures that all cuts remain straight.

2. Fold the fabric in half along the lengthwise grain. Align the selvage edges rather than matching the cut edges on either end.

3. Place the folded edge closest to you and align it with a horizontal line on your cutting mat.

4. Align a rotary-cutting ruler with a vertical line on the cutting mat, near the cut edge of the fabric. Cut along the ruler's edge with a rotary cutter. If you're left-handed, reverse the illustration and cut along the left side of the ruler.

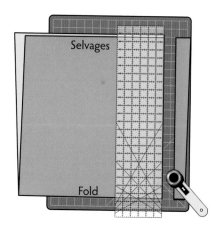

MACHINE PIECING

Accuracy is extremely important when piecing. The seam allowance is always ¼" unless otherwise indicated in the project instructions. Most sewing machines have a presser foot that measures ¼" from the needle to the right edge; if you have a ¼" foot, use it to gauge your seam allowances. If not, lower the needle and measure ¼" to the right of the needle; lay a piece of masking tape on the sewing-machine bed to indicate the seam allowance.

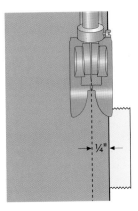

Other tips for machine piecing include:

- Sew with the right sides of the fabric pieces together.
- Pin the pieces together if necessary for accuracy.
- Save time and thread by chain piecing.
- Piecing some blocks leaves the ends of the seam allowances extending past the block edges. Trim these "wings" or "dog-ears" even with the block edges.

PRESSING

There is a difference between pressing and ironing. While ironing involves a gliding motion and heavy pressure, pressing is accomplished with a gentle up-and-down motion that's less likely to distort the fabric. When quilting, be sure to press!

- Use a steam iron on the cotton setting.
- Press after sewing each seam.
- Seam allowances are generally pressed to one side—usually toward the darker fabric. However, some situations dictate alternate pressing. The goals are always to reduce bulk, prevent dark fabrics from showing through light fabrics on the front of the quilt, and allow the quilt top to lie flat.

CHOOSING BATTING

Choosing batting for your quilt depends on your personal preference for its finished appearance and the desired warmth. Here are some guidelines for batting selection:

- Traditional batting is 100% cotton and lends a most delicious crinkly texture once the completed quilt is washed. Plus, being cotton, it can be laundered in a standard household washer and dryer without additional care.
- Cotton batting grips other quilt layers and helps prevent shifting during quilting.
- Wool and silk battings can offer exceptional warmth but may require special washing or dry cleaning. Check the manufacturer's care instructions to be sure.

Color Counts

If your quilt top includes lots of whites or light-colored fabrics, use a bleached white batting. A natural, unbleached batting will alter the bright whiteness of your quilt top. Similarly, if your quilt top consists primarily of black or other dark colors, consider using a black batting.

BASTING

Whether you choose to tie, hand quilt, or machine quilt your finished project, proper basting assures that the quilt top, batting, and backing don't shift, wrinkle, or fold over during the quilting process. There are several different ways to baste a quilt including pin basting, spray basting, thread basting, and even plastic-tack basting. I prefer the pin-basting method described here.

1. Examine the wrong side of the quilt top carefully and trim any stray threads that may be visible through the light fabrics of the quilt top.

2. Press the quilt top if necessary to remove wrinkles and creases or flatten bulky areas.

3. Place the backing fabric wrong side up on a flat surface large enough to accommodate the entire quilt.

4. Use masking tape to secure the edges of the backing fabric to the surface. Pull the backing taut but avoid stretching it.

5. Place the batting on top of the backing and smooth gently from the center outward to the edges. The entire surface should be smooth, without ridges, wrinkles, or bumps.

6. Center the quilt top right side up over the batting.

7. Using rustproof safety pins made specifically for quilters, pin all three layers of the quilt sandwich together. Space the pins about 5" apart, beginning at the center and working toward the outer edges.

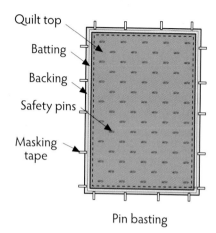

Quilt top
Batting
Backing
Safety pins
Masking tape

Pin basting

8. Remove the tape and you're ready to quilt.

Leave It to Long Arm

If you plan to hire a long-arm machine quilter to quilt your project, no basting on your part is required. Ask your quilter how the quilt top, batting, and backing should be prepared; generally, the backing and batting should be 4" larger than the quilt top on all sides. This helps the quilter load the layers onto the quilting frame properly.

QUILTING

The word *quilting* is often used as a catchall term to describe the craft of making a quilt. However, quilting is specifically the act of stitching together the layers of the quilt sandwich. Quilting is functional, as it secures the layers of the quilt together and prevents shifting, ultimately making the finished quilt stronger and more durable. But quilting can be decorative as well, complementing the quilt design or becoming a feature in its own right. Whether you choose hand quilting, hand tying, quilting on your home sewing machine, or long-arm machine quilting, your choices of thread, color, and pattern make your quilt unique.

BINDING

Binding is the last step toward completion of a quilt and it's no secret that it's absolutely my favorite part of the process. I love everything from choosing the fabric for the binding to making the binding, attaching it, and then hand sewing it to the back. I think it has something to do with being able to sit under the quilt while I stitch.

The binding is the narrow strip of fabric at the outermost edge of the quilt that finishes the quilt by covering the raw edges. But it's more than that: it's the frame around the picture.

Choose quality fabric of 100% quilter's cotton for binding your quilt. The binding will be handled and pulled and tugged often during its service and must be strong and durable.

1. Cut 2½" x 42" strips of binding fabric as instructed for your project. With right sides together, lay one strip on the other at a 90° angle as shown. Sew across the overlapped area along the diagonal.

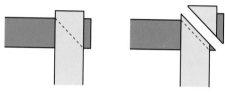

Joining strips

2. Trim the excess fabric ¼" from the seam and press the seam allowances open.

Press seam allowances open.

3. Repeat steps 1 and 2 until all the strips are sewn together. Press the entire length in half with wrong sides together.

4. Working from the right side of the quilt, align the raw edge of the binding with the quilt's raw edge. Leave an 8" to 10" length of binding free at the start; when you have sewn the binding around the entire perimeter of your quilt, this tail will allow you the necessary work space to finish the binding.

5. Sew the binding to the quilt with a ¼" seam allowance. Stop sewing ¼" from the first corner.

Backstitch, clip the threads, and remove the quilt from your machine.

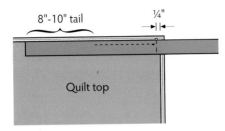

8"-10" tail   ¼"

Quilt top

6. Turn the quilt into position to sew the binding onto the next side of the quilt. Fold the binding up and then back down on itself, keeping the raw edges aligned. Resume stitching at the corner. This will create a miter at the corner.

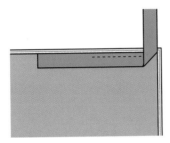

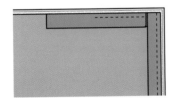

7. Continue sewing around the quilt, mitering the binding at each corner, until you are about 20" away from where you began. Backstitch, clip the threads, and remove the quilt from your machine.

8. Overlap the ends of the binding strip. Mark the trailing end, leaving a ½" overlap, and cut off the excess binding.

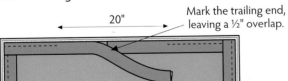

20"   Mark the trailing end, leaving a ½" overlap.

½" overlap

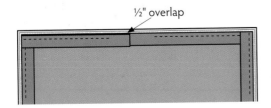

9. Unfold both ends of the binding and align the raw edges with right sides together. Stitch, using a ¼" seam allowance, to join the binding ends.

10. Press the seam allowances open. Refold the joined binding, align the raw edges with the quilt edge, and stitch into place.

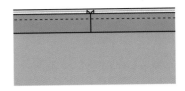

11. Fold the binding to the back of the quilt, covering the raw edges, so that the binding fold just covers the binding seam line. Blindstitch the binding to the backing by hand, using a thread color that matches the binding fabric.

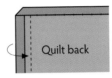
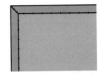

Quilt back

Blind-Stitch Basics

A blind stitch is a nearly invisible option for attaching the binding to the back of a quilt. Begin by tying a knot in the thread and stitching through the backing seam allowance, allowing the knot and thread to be hidden in the finished quilt.

Bring the needle to the right side through the fold of the binding (1). Take a tiny stitch into the quilt backing (2), emerging ⅛" to ¼" away, in position for the next stitch (3).

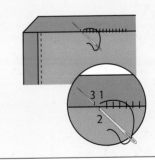

about the author

I'm a wife, mother of two daughters, soapmaker, photographer, thrifter, long-time blogger, and self-taught quilter. When I'm not shuttling kids to and fro, tending my garden, or locking my family out of the car and making them dance to gain entry, I'm usually at my sewing machine . . . or scheming to find my way there as soon as possible.

I have distinct memories of my mother sitting at her sewing machine when I was a child. I can still hear the hum of her machine echoing in mine as I sew. Couple that memory with the groovy patchwork and rickrack wallpaper I had in my childhood bedroom, and I know the very roots of my love for quilting.

Visit me online at www.oldredbarnco.blogspot.com where you can find out what I'm designing, sewing, quilting, and possibly even pondering.

acknowledgments

A special thank-you to my mother-in-law, Sara Bolyard, for recognizing my love of quilts and encouraging me to give it a go. She sat, more than once, teaching this skittish pattern reader and fabric cutter the tricks of the trade.

Thank you to Russ and Rhonda Adams of the Back Porch Quilters for your friend-ship and fabulous quilting. Visit their website at www.thebackporchquilters.com.

Thank you to quilt fabric and supply manufacturers that provide an array of products and fabric design choices to please every taste. Your quality products ensure that my quilts will stand the test of time. My favorites are Moda, Robert Kaufman, Riley Blake, Michael Miller, Windham, Art Gallery, Hobbs Heirloom Collection Batting, and Aurifil Thread.

And finally, a huge shout-out to the amazing online quilting community that shares so freely. When I meet one of you in real life, you never disappoint. You're kind, supportive, funny, and wildly creative. Even if I haven't met you in person (yet!), I know that if given the chance we'd be fast friends. Thank you so much.